10 Steps to Achieve any Outcomes you Desire!

Build the LIFE you LOVE to LIVE

Why use the 10 Steps Program?

We begin to make change for the better & we continue that change for the better, then only betterment can ensue. You can achieve your dreams if you never give up reaching for your dreams.

These 10 Steps are a given process that allows to believe those dreams are within reach & offers a process that allows you to attain those dreams. Once you begin to attain your dreams, you will realize that more dreams are possible. By building those dreams, you have already begun to Build a LIFE you LOVE to LIVE! (tm)

Join the Journey with LIVE & LOVE LIFE FB

rjhorner@live-love-life.ca

10 Steps to Achieve any Outcomes you Desire: A process to Build the LIFE of your Dreams!

By: Robert J Horner

Writer, Speaker, LIFE Coach & Motivator of Mankind!

Printed in Canada

I would like to thank my wife, Maria Fatima Horner for all her support & guidance & her tolerance with me throughout our time together. Nothing I could ever do to make up for the bad times we had & the time spent away from her while working on this project.

Thanks also to all the Mentors, Trainers & Educators who have made me who I am. Your guidance & input has been invaluable to my LIFE!

A special Thanks to my former Boss & Mentor, Brent McKee. You were the one who allowed me to change my LIFE. You stood by me when few would. You offered your guidance, some kind words & deep hearted mentorship that helped me realize who I should be.

Table of Contents

Chapter 1

KNOW, LIKE & TRUST ME!

I want you to get to know me, so that you will know that I am an honorable man of honesty & Integrity who treats people well, for the most part. Let's be honest, nobody's perfect. Certainly not me.

I believe you should…

"HIT people with all you got. Treat people with Honesty, Integrity & Tact (H.I.T.)." ~RJ Horner

I am a family man of a blended family. As a second family…Stepfather to 2 kids from very good parents who were very much quality parents but just could not seem to go as a couple.

In this environment, I might have been an interference to their LIFE & a barrier to any potential for a happy reconciliation with their parents. Which until I came into the picture would always remain a possibility in a child's eyes. Every child must wish for their parents to be together, for a happy family. I did for many years, even when I was beginning to accept that my parents just couldn't get along.

Now I have a family that does not truly belong to me, as much as I tried to implant myself, they still see me as the man who married their mother. I married their mother after all, not them. Regardless of the work I have done to build a home for them, I am always the odd man out. It's a role I accept. I am still an outsider, but I will say that I have now been with that family for over 15 years, it is my family. I have earned the right to say that, as a "Step-Dad".

Like anyone you might see on a stage who spins a tale or puts on a show, their LIFE is not all it may appear to be. The perfect LIFE they want us to see, does not really exist. Even the best of them, still stub their toes or get up on the wrong side of the bed. They lose people or have hardship hit them like anyone else.

These professionals will want you to know that they have their shit together, so that you might better rely on them for their source of enlightenment. Again, that LIFE they would have you imagine they are LIVING is quite possibly false. You must trust your own judgement for all characters you meet & all deals you make. It is YOUR LIFE after all.

Speaking for myself, I can certainly state with all passion, fire & affection, as a man of integrity that I am not perfect.

Affirmation: "I am not perfect, never will be, but I am amazing."

I do not always get it right. Fact is I get it wrong…often enough. If you ask my wife that's "95% of the time.", but she also holds her tongue 93% of the time too…so that gives me a 7% chance at getting it right.

As I unravel this document…This is the Official 1st Edition

YOU will begin to understand a couple of things about my LIFE that will make your LIFE a little easier for you. You will learn a lot more about ME! Not that I am all that important! At least not any more important than you, nor as important as the fact that you have come across this information & are now privy to such wisdom…all are equally as important.

You will begin to learn more about yourself through the eyes of others, through my observations, for I am an empath…I see things about people that others do not. Through the eyes, ears, body, soul & verse (the five senses), I see into the hearts of many…& the few.

YOU may begin to learn a thing or two that I've been fortunate to have learned from the masters, of which I have taken from all they have learned…even though I haven't learned ALL they know from them ALL, & never will. They were generous enough to SHARE THE WISDOM!   It would be selfish of me not to SHARE THE WISDOM with others.

Though I could never learn ALL that these masters have learned, that doesn't stop me from seeking out more wisdom, but I have accumulated so much that I absolutely must share it, lest I burst.

I don't want to burst! There is so much I want to do yet; "We've only just begun…" a tune that rings in my ear every time I think of life ending short.

I have only begun to realize that I can teach you things through my words, my enthusiasm for knowledge & my passion to share.

I used to hate reading Non-Fiction books as a kid. Most of them were boring as textbooks. How enthusiastic were you to read **them**?

I hated textbooks.

I almost didn't read *Lord of the Flies;* until someone began talking about the rebellion forming & the killing(s), what? In a high-school book? Oh, I loved to read. I am a nerd…as my wife likes to call me. (I'm sure it's a term of endearment.)

The thing is, I have always been a nerd. As a child, I thought I would have become a teacher. The problem with that is people called me a nerd. Early on people called me two things; "Nerd!" & "Queer!" Well there was another word for it, but I won't bother with it here, I'm sure you can guess what it is.

There were kids who thought I was gay, because I soft & sensitive. That was something I thankfully learned people thought of me early on & rather than take it to heart, or maybe I did. As an adult I eventually needed to speak to a counsellor, I am rather proud to admit; The experience(s) changed me & my LIFE forever!

Well, I am a nerd! I will admit that, though I am quite confident I am not gay, ("Not that there's anything wrong with that!" ~ Jerry Seinfeld)

…though as a matter of integrity I will let you in on a not so scary secret that I have little use to tell people about, yet it could put me in a bad light in some people's eyes. Some might say it is taboo & downright frowned upon.

Here's the thing! I am a reader, a writer & editor of erotic fiction novels & a purveyor of all things…erotica, in print or recorded format.

How's that for getting it wrong? I mean porn! Really?

I know…I've lost some followers already, just for stating that for the record, but I am a man of integrity & what good would I be if I kept that little piece of information secret. Well, the people who abandon me because of my inclinations aren't the people I am here to lead.

I am available to lead the ones who get it wrong, the people who find the need to explain who they are, or that they think differently than you or me, or any other individual. Quite likely, they don't feel like an individual at all. They can't reconcile their lives to exist peaceably with others.

As for porn? As a young mind impressionable & prone to reading, I was exposed (Tee-Hee!) to 2 things literary early on in my influential pubescent years.

> 1. *The Joy of Sex* - though I do not like textbooks, this one proved to be quite useful. If only to myself for quite a while, but I did learn most of what I know about sex from that book.

I also think it made me a masterful lover. I learned about anatomy, the human body & sexuality from this one book.

2. Then I found & read my first ***Penthouse Forum***. Stories about Sex? "OMG" …Oh yeah, 80's child. "Oh My God!" (You can see why some people might have thought I was gay, don't you?) That was it. I was hooked! Sex…in words! I was in awe & I never stopped reading ever since. Over 30 years.

They say if you study something long enough you become a master at it. Well?? Get your mind off that. Ok, I am a master lover. I have most certainly studied love, lust & erotic behaviour.

I believed them at the beginning when the videos said, "This material is for educational purposes ONLY!"

I learned all I could! 'Course I also believed them when they said that unlawful recording of this material was punishable by a fine of up to $5000 & 10 Yrs. of imprisonment, so…! (…Grain of salt)

If I am a man of integrity as I claim to be, then how can I proport to state that a man who knows & likes porn could be a man who is honest & trustworthy, much less tactful? (Well, that tactful part does take work)

Chapter 2

NO EXCUSES!

I have been given a gift of curiosity through the written word. I was also given the gift of the book(s) that just happen to fall into my lap…& I do have a love of reading. I most certainly took advantage of those gifts, I tell you.

Oh yes, I did…I learned all I could. Especially when these video tape (VHS) things came out when I was older. I decided to maximize my potential for knowledge. They did say it was "education purposes" after all. Then came computers & the internet. Boom! Exponential Knowledge!

Integrity is not just a word you speak or write down on paper. It is a value you LIVE!

I believe I LIVE the value of integrity & I will go one further step to ease your mind that I stand by my convictions, though I may have lost some people who will already believe that because I like porn I am less than nothing.

I am not here to prove anything to them, only to show others that though they may make lousy choices sometimes, they may hold their head high & stand tall as a person of integrity.

(Look up Integrity if you don't believe you could be somebody!)

I mentioned earlier that not only do I read, but I write Erotic Fiction Novels. I also stated that though I admit I am Nerd…I'm confident I am not gay. I must admit though that if I did not at least imagine or picture a penis, then I wouldn't be a very good writer. At least at erotica & my wife thinks I am pretty good. Enough that I might Actually have a story here, you know…that kind of commitment to the craft.

The point is my wife knows who I am & she is proud of me. That matters more to me then the opinion of those who might sour in hearing of my affliction, addiction, what? Truth is, I don't care. There are times that I enjoy Erotica in one form or another with & without my partner & lover. She is proud of me, supports me & stands by me. Hers is truly the only opinion that matters to me.

OK! Don't you run away so fast. Your opinion matters too. What I am trying to say is…

I am a man of integrity because I am whole in who I am, what I believe & how I behave. I do what I do & I stand by what I believe in. I don't always do what I say I will (My biggest Failing). I admit when I am wrong & take 100% responsibility for my LIFE!

I am RJ Horner:
I know who I am!
I know where I am going!
I know what I doing to get there!

It took me a long time to be able to say that…& believe that about Myself! Many hours of getting in touch with, listening to & learning about Myself.

LIFE is harsh. Mine certainly was, at least that's what I would have you believe. Heck, that's what I believe, and that's all that matters right. What we believe ourselves is more important than the opinion of any other person we might know or even trust. It is so important that we argue with anyone who dares tell us otherwise.

LIFE as I have LIVED it was most certainly harsh. My troubled past. My downtrodden circumstance. Burdened by debt, boggled by depression, riddled with despair. The world was out to get me. LIFE was out to get me. Hell, I used to quip not overly sarcastic that, "Darwin had me in mind…Whatever can go wrong, will go wrong." …with my LIFE.

Try as I might see it otherwise. Whatever circumstances I faced would bring about some dreary and sad tale of misery. OK. I am spinning a yarn of bold and brash colour, but was it really so bad? I guess it is all in perception, and I couldn't see past the muck and grime building up on my windshield as I struggled to see through it. I tried to imagine and hope for better days, but they seemed some far off and distant land.

Oh, there were good times and they would come in stages, never knowing when the fuse would burn low as it always did. It was just a matter of time before it all blew up. No one knew what would set it off or when.

Was it a fuse, maybe a timer…spontaneous combustion?

If there were some way to predict its inevitable explosion, we might better prepare for the coming days. It was like trying to predict a tornado. Oh, that is possible now? Well, so is my temper.

Yeah, I make my LIFE sound like a natural disaster that could not be avoided, a coming calamity of epic proportion. Some days it seemed as if that was what it was. There was always trouble on the horizon. In the aftermath, when all the dust had settled and life was getting smoothed over again, my wife would begrudgingly state, "Its ok, I forgive you…until next time."

That is no way to live. "…until next time."

Knowing that one day (no one knew when or why), the twister would come twirling through again leaving destruction in its wake. When she offered this little stab, it had the Desired effect. It went straight to my heart. It hurt like hell, and it was meant to. Yet knowing how she felt and the burden she was to bear, could not change the Outcomes any more than knowing that she was absolutely right. Someday the tide would turn and overcome us again.

This description of LIFE as we knew it was meant for you to feel my pain. Not just my pain but that of my support system as well. It was a terrible pain…of knowing I was troubled and unhappy; of knowing that I was an uncontrollable beast. I am reminded of the Rolling Stones song… "I'll never be your beast of burden." Yet that was me all right, causing strife and discomfort for those that knew and might love me. Makes me sad to think that is what I offer my woman…A Beast of Burden.

The theme song for my LIFE at that time though might just as well have been that Johnny Cash favorite,

Ring of Fire:
"I'm going down, down, down in a burning ring of fire.
Going down, down, down and the flame is getting higher.
Oh, it burns, burns, burns in the ring of fire. The ring of fire."

You see I know it so well because I used to sing it as I fell in my despair. It was painful that I was so aware of my trouble yet could do nothing to alter my reality.

It does make me laugh to know that this song could also be used as the theme song for a hemorrhoid commercial. (Sing the song again now and tell me you don't see it.)

I bring that up because I would often snip when people would peeve me off, "Did I ever tell you how much you remind me of a hemorrhoid…a terrible pain in the ass." I was in a state and I didn't care who might know it. I didn't want to know it, didn't care to hear it. C'est la vie.

I've come a long way from who I was to where I am now!

I know who I am. I want to help YOU know who YOU are!

That is why I am so passionate & so caring & I truly want YOU to KNOW; LIKE & TRUST me! That means getting to know you as you get to know me. The only way I can help anyone is to get to know them, who they are, what they need & what drives them.

"People don't care how much you know until you know how much you care!"

I care…because I have been there!

You will learn that. You will learn to trust me as I tell you some of my exploits that help us all to grow. The purpose of all LIFE is to grow. I have learned that much & I intend to #SHARE that with YOU.

I would like you to believe, ONLY because I believe it myself, that I am a man whom you can trust & I believe I have skills & knowledge that will prove useful to YOU in YOUR Future. I have information, I have Wisdom to spare, to #SHARE…I have to SHARE THE WISDOM!

…& if I have it to spare then to me it is abundant.

WOW!

"Profound!" As my Friend & Mentor Amit Ambegaonkar would say.

I say it again. Profound! Yeah? If I have it to spare than to me, it is abundant!

Chapter 3

#SHAREABUNDANCE

Why is *#shareabundance* such a Powerful statement? **(Pause for effect)**

Oh! Those were behind the scenes notes…how embarrassing! We will discuss Abundance shortly, but…

If I have something to spare, then to ME it's abundant. Here is some more profound thinking; If I have something in abundance, shouldn't I #SHARE it?

If I had something in abundance & I didn't #SHARE it, then I would be selfish & greedy for not sharing. If I can #SHARE something of value to you, the wisdom I have accumulated into some reasonably discernable information, I can take what I have learned & #SHARE it.

Several years ago, began a journey that would take me from the lowest depths on a climb to peaks that were unimaginable to me at the time. When you feel down and out and just can't see anyway to regain control, it is almost impossible to believe that life could get better, much less that it might Actually be enjoyable. You are just trying to survive and can't believe it's possible to thrive.

Oh, I'm not there. Not yet anyway, but I do believe it's possible. Not only do I believe it, but I have faith that it is going to happen…soon. I could never in a million years have thought that I would Achieve what I am going to tell you next, but I am on the precipice of financial stability. By the time you read this I am confident that I will have gained control of the last element of life balance that was beyond my means. I will likely be financially solvent. That is my hope anyway, and I have faith.

That is also something I couldn't say until very recently. "I have faith." Those words were blasphemy to me. To think something was possible; to believe something might happen; to believe that I deserved something like that?

Impossible!

I used to say, "I have faith! I have faith that every single person will do what is in their best interest to do."

It was a sad statement I know but that is how I felt at the time. I can now look back on those times and shake my head at the person I had become.

I used to have the words of others ringing in my head, though I am sure now that they were imagined voices.

"Who do you think you are?"

"What, you think you're somebody important?"

"You want to be somebody?" "Yeah, right!"

"You think you're better than us?"

That kept reinforcing my negative beliefs. I didn't know how to answer those voices at the time and they just kept putting me down and keeping me there.

"You're low class, the lowest of the low."

"Get down and stay down, that is where you belong anyway; in the gutter." Such was my state of mind.

Yep, I had a long way to go on my journey of personal and spiritual growth. That was another problem I had was embracing spirituality, but that is a discussion for another book.

One term I keep hearing in the personal development circles is abundance. It keeps resurfacing and some of you may know what it refers to. Abundance has become known as the idea that there is more than enough of everything to go around, that every single one of us can have everything our hearts Desire, that no matter whether it is money, food, clothes, housing and other resources there is more than enough. There is an abundant supply.

If there is an abundant supply of everything, then why do we not have more of everything individually? We could get into the discussion and we could debate this on both sides of the table for generations to come. Some people believe it is our political systems that exists to keep the workers in their place. Others believe that it is our economic systems that are not built to encourage us to Achieve our Dreams, that the American Dream is just that; a Dream.

Chapter 4

ABUNDANCE

In the circles of Personal Development, you begin to hear certain terms resurfacing often. These terms are reiterated this often to motivate you and give you hope. It is in this spirit that I offer you hope, except it is more than just hope. It is a strategy. In fact, those same self-help gurus tell you that hope is not a way of life or, "Hope is not a strategy."

If you hope for anything to happen for you, then you have to go out and make it happen. You have to plan for the life you want. If you want a dynamic career, a happy prosperous home, financial freedom or to own your own business essentially being your own boss, it is entirely up to you to make it happen. You must create a strategy and come up with a plan.

One term I kept hearing in the personal development circles is abundance. It keeps resurfacing and some of you may know what it refers to. Abundance has become known as the idea that there is more than enough of everything to go around, that every single one of us can have everything our hearts Desire, that no matter whether it is money, food, clothes, housing and other resources there is more than enough. There is an abundant supply.

What is abundance?

Merriam-Webster Dictionary defines abundance as:

- An ample quantity
- Profusion;
    - Lavish expenditure or extravagance
    - The quality or state of being profuse
    - Great quantity, lavish display or supply
- Affluence, wealth
    - An abundant flow or supply
    - A flowing to or toward a point
- Relative degree of plentifulness

This term abundance often arises in conjunction with the Law of Attraction. As you can see it refers to having more than enough of the things you Desire. I have taken the study of abundance a step further when Bob Proctor recommended that if you want to understand the Law of Attraction you should make a study of the other Universal Laws and how to apply them. This led me on a mission to discover some of these Universal laws.

It was how I rediscovered spirituality.

There are many laws that govern the Universe and our existence but the most prevalent of these is the Law of Attraction, which states that like attracts like.

- If you emit negative vibrations or thoughts, then you will receive negativity in response.
- If you have any hope to attract positivity, then you must remain Positive and only allow those Positive vibrations to dominate your thinking.
- If you start to move toward that which you Desire like money or happiness, in essence abundance then the Universe will place more of those things before you bringing you even more of the good things in life.
- However, if you are filled with anger, hate, resentment and jealousy, guess what the Universe will provide. (Trust me on this one I can offer personal experience)

If there is an abundant supply of everything then, why do we not have more individually?

We could get into the discussion and we could debate this on both sides of the table for generations to come. Some people believe it is our political systems that exists to keep the workers in their place. Others believe that it is our economic systems that are not built to encourage us to Achieve our Dreams, that the American Dream is just that; a Dream!

The Universal Laws have an answer for that too and we will discuss this before the end of the book.

Having said that, we are told far too often that the world is unfair by those we are surrounded by. Our friends, family and supportive figures all tell us the same things. We are all broke, or most of us anyway, no one really has any money. We all have debt. That's just the way it is. 5% of the population holds 95% of the wealth. What? Really? Like I said, LIFE is unfair.

You cannot possibly hope to gain all your heart Desires with just a basic understanding of the Law of Attraction. It is just an entry point into the understanding of how to Achieve everything you want in life. The other natural laws of the Universe demonstrate how to have dominion over your LIFE and your Dreams. Dreams that are achievable by each and every one of us.

The message they circulate in the personal development circles will lead you to believe that it is possible for you to succeed.

Do you believe them?

Do you believe in yourself?

That is why personal development is big business, because you do not believe in yourself. But they really do want to help you Achieve wealth and abundance.

They do that by helping you believe in yourself. Why? Because if you do better, then the Universe fairs better. But you can do better. It is all up to you. You can do it if you try. You just need to Analyze your life; your hopes; your Dreams. Turn those Dreams into goals and you are on your way. You cannot help but succeed it you know what you are going after.

(That is another of those Laws of which I speak. We will not get into that. It is not what this book is about. Research the Natural Laws of the Universe.)

OK. It is more difficult than that but if you just start working toward your wants via micro-goals based on long-term goals, you will find that LIFE has a way of working itself out, leading you toward your goals. I used to be skeptical of this, but I have found it to be true that if you just take steps with definite purpose in the direction of your Desire, those things you need will show up in your path.

This book is in reference to that definite purpose. It befalls me to tell this story because of my Desire for more; to be more; to do more; to become more.

This book began when I truly wanted more, not only for me but for everyone. Again, another Natural Law of the Universe that held me hostage until I was ready to embrace it. Throughout this discussion of the Law of Abundance I have Actually opened your eyes to several of the Laws. Within the pages ahead we will open up that discussion further.

There is another factor that has literally kept me from achieving my Dreams that takes effect at this point. It is the reason I mention it now. The Law of Action states that you cannot hope to Achieve your Dreams if you do not Act. The Universe will put those things you need in your path but if you fail to Act, no one can be blamed for your lack of success but you. Without the Law of Action, the Law of Attraction would be useless.

This will be discussed further in later chapters, but I am here to tell you that we can change the world. We can change the status quo if we just take steps to make that change. If you truly want that change then you must take the necessary steps to Achieve that change. You must take necessary Action, but there is one and only one person you must convince.

It is up to you. It is up to me. It is up to all of us to work for all of us. Do you want to make that change? I want to make that change.

"Be the change you want to see in the world." ~
Mohandas K Ghandi

The second quote may be familiar to some of you. Those words were delivered by a man who was way ahead of his time and never truly found his place in the world. So much so that he created his own world in Neverland. He didn't want to grow up, thus he never really did. He refused to conform to what the world wanted him to be, but he never stopped making a difference. He never stopped trying to change the world. They say you never know what you had until it is gone. Well I can attest to that. I miss that man and the genius he gave to us.

Michael Jackson was a genius who LIVED LIFE according to how he saw the world, or rather, how he wanted to see it. Michael Jackson believed that the Universe was larger than any one of us. He lived according to his own vision and walked his own path. He was so powerful and influential that people just went along with his extravagant and eclectic Dreams. I envy that way of life and truly miss that man. I can only hope that people never forget what he gave us, therefore what he left for us. That man had a legacy that was missed because of his eccentrics. It is impossible to know what would have become of his visions if only people saw what he saw.

 Better yet, Michael Jackson had abundance. Here is a man that had so much financial abundance that he bought his own castle and built his own personal theme park. He Dreamed big and he lived big. You too can live big, but you just have to want it.

There are other factors that will need to be in place for your Desires to come true. We will discuss them through this process, but I wanted you to understand the term of abundance before we moved forward with our journey to create a Better World.

I know that I want abundance & abundant LIVING. I am sure that most everyone wants abundance, but they just don't do anything more than wish for it.

If you want more than you have right now, then you must go out there and get it. You must strive to Achieve if you want your Dreams to come true. If I want my Dreams come true, then I am responsible to make it happen. The same goes for each of you. Whatever you want in life must come from you.

"I'm starting with the man in the mirror. I'm asking him to change his ways, and no message could have been any clearer. If you want to make the world a better place, take a look at yourself, and make that change." ~ Michael Jackson

If we want to make the world a better place, then we must make the change. The more of us that make the change the sooner we might realize this Dream of abundance. The path to abundance begins with what we learned in kindergarten. We can have it all if we just share it all. #SHARETHEWISDOM #SHARETHEWEALTH #SHARETHELOVE

Wisdom

Wealth

LOVE

Of these three things the world has in abundance, there is more than enough to go around, if we just remember what we were taught early on in life. As more of us begin to share these abundant supplies, there will be more to spread to others. They will continue a path that will begin to make a change. It will set off a chain reaction of events that will begin a new era. If we SHARE Abundance, we create a Better World.

Chapter 5

Who am I?

I am Robert John Horner:
I know who I am!
I know where I am going!
I know what I am doing to get there!

Most importantly, I am going there!

I am taking all those I can, if they are willing to go along for the ride. It could be quite an adventure. There's safety in numbers, so we should be quite strong on this journey together.

I know I have some things to #SHARE! I am humble enough not to believe for a second with any value to offer others. There are Millions of people that we are connected to who have talents, wisdom, skills & lore to #SHARE in the abundance of wisdom, wealth & love that is available to us all, to be passed around & used by us all, together.

I know I am starting to sound like some hooky guru-type spouting Peace, Love & Harmony.

I hope I can eventually make you see that my sanity is never in question, though my choices may occasionally be. I am a level-headed guy (most of the time; Sorry!) who has LIVED a LIFE! I have learned a few things on my journey & I have also learned that this Wisdom, Wealth & LOVE, of which are available in ABUNDANCE are selfish of you to keep to yourself & only hold value when you #SHARE them.

I intend to #SHARE these with you as I not only encourage but inspire & empower you to utilize them to Build a Better World for yourself & others. I also implore you to #SHARE these abundant resources with others...ASAP!

Now Damn IT! GO!

Who are YOU? Let's get to know YOU!

To enable yourself to move on, you must get to know yourself.

- What do you value?
- What do you believe in?
- What do you stand for?
- How do you like to be treated?
- Do you show people how to treat you?
- Do you say nothing, which speaks volumes?
- Do you have religious affiliations principles?
- Moralistic & principled, yet not religious?
- Agnostic? Atheist?
- Are you of little faith, perhaps some bad habits?
- Perhaps you are of little morals

Maybe, you are an asshole! Some of the signs are:
- people have told you about your Attitude or behaviour

- few people want to be around you;

- you might not even know this about yourself,

- "I'm really a nice guy, people just…"

You recognize the signs. If you are unstable & not at peace in any way, these signs will bring forth some familiarity. You can see them in yourself.

You are who you are, right?

I want to get to know you.

What do you do? What would you like to do? What makes you tick?

What do you Dream about? What are your Dreams?

What do you envision for your future?

You do have Dreams, don't you? All of your Dreams have come true! Really, then why are you unhappy?

If you were content with who you are, then why do you still get upset, angry, frustrated?

There is ONLY one reason. You want more!

You want something else! You want a better Outcomes! You think it is possible, at least your mind tells you so, that you can have more, otherwise you would not & could not hope for another possibility, one that is better than your current circumstance.

If we could not imagine more, then you could not hope for more. There is more out there! We have been shown that there is more, so we want more. We hope for more, but we just cannot seem to get more.

What do we do for more? Some of us will do tremendous things for more…to have more.

Some of us will resort to immoral Acts to Achieve more. Some will even walk on anyone who gets in their way of more.

You can be corrupt in your endeavors & you may enjoy it while it lasts, but a house of cards cannot stand forever. A structure with solid foundations however can withhold the tests of time.

Others, once they have become enlightened on the subject, will begin to add value to receive more. This is the path I have learned & I have begun to walk an easier step. The path of service to others.

We want more, that much is obvious, but why can't we have more?

Again, there is ONLY one answer to the question. We cannot have what we do not try to get.

As Wayne Gretzky puts it,

"You miss 100% of the shots you don't take!"

You must be more than willing to put it out there, put yourself out there, to get something back. You must take some form of Action! You must give something to get something. These are not just clichés. They are a means of LIVING that will lead you to adopt & express an Attitude of success.

I have heard it time & again, "Those who don't succeed, usually are the ones who don't take Action." I thought that I was implementing this practice. I thought I was Acting…After hearing these speakers, I began to make changes in my LIFE, yet never took significant Action. I would always take safe Actions, small steps toward making progress, setting myself up for success, never changing who I was on the inside.

"Take Decisive Action!" This is the voice I hear over & over again.

I began to struggle with where I was failing to take significant Action, I mean I had all these Dreams…

I just wasn't following through on them. Even one project that I worked on for more than a couple of years failed to produce any value because I was always putting myself out there at a safe distance from consequence. I wasn't getting involved in the process, or even involved enough in the community I hoped to serve.

I could see areas in my LIFE & my projects that needed a steady hand, a solid foundation or a coordinated effort. I could see that somebody needed to do something to change things. Oh, I hate that choice of words. It often inspires me to Action.

I hate when somebody says, "Somebody should do something about that!"

"Aren't you a somebody then?" Would often be my heated & sarcastic reply.

We are ALL somebodies! We can ALL do something…about anything! We can ALL stand up & take Action on any principle or belief we rely heavily on. We can ALL have more involvement in our home, our families & especially in the community we hope to serve. We can be somebody!

I have said it before & I say it again now; I want to change the world! That is something you should know about me.

"Isn't it strange that those who think they are crazy enough to change the world, are often the ones that do."
~ Steve Jobs

They say, "People don't care how much you know until they know how much you care." I also used to say, when frustrated, "I don't care." My boss caught me, stopped me short on that one time & I now cannot help but use the expression. This is the same man who taught me the line, "Aren't you a Somebody then? It was a short eye-opening conversation.

The conversation went as follows…

"I don't Care!" I stated with frustration.

"You absolutely do care, & I can prove it with one sentence" My boss's reply.

"OK, Prove it!"

"If you didn't care you wouldn't get upset." Wow! Profound!

I was stunned while seeking for an answer to that retort. He had put me in my place, with just one simple statement. You must understand that this was a man I respected enough to be brutally honest with me…even if it hurts. So, he ever so gently & tactfully offered up guidance that was direct & motivating without being overt & malicious.

To this day I can no longer allow myself to utter the words, "I don't care!"

I care enough to want my own LIFE to be better. I care enough to make my wife's LIFE better. I care enough to make my environment & the LIVES of those around me better. I care enough to want to change the world to make my environment & the LIVES of those around me better.

I care! Enough that I must be somebody & do something to change the world as I know it.

I want to change the world! I want to make my LIFE better. I can make MY LIFE better by helping make others S better.

Chapter 6

My Path to Achievement

"Desire is the Starting Point of All Achievement." ~ Napoleon Hill

Do you have a Desire? Like the great Dr. Martin Luther King, do you have a Dream? Do you have a Dream that is left unfulfilled? If you do, you are not LIVING the LIFE you truly want.

Do you want to Achieve that Dream? Then you have some choices to make. One of those choices is whether to Act on your Dreams. Another might be to take some steps toward the LIFE you want.

What do you want? Decide! Then go get what you want!

It really is that simple!

I'm sure you do not believe that. If you did, achieving your Dreams would be easy. You would be doing so already. If you are achieving your Dreams, then the odds are you would not be reading this book. You cannot or do not know how to do it alone.

Courtesy of Jack Canfield, from *The Success Principles*. Here is the simplest formula for achieving your Desired Outcomes.

E + R = O

(E)VENTS +

(R)ESPONSES =
(O)UTCOMES

You have also heard the explanation of this formula from Newton's Third Law,

"For every Action there is an equal & opposite reaction."

This also represents the above formula quite nicely. Every Action brings about some reaction or Outcomes. You commit an Act, that Act creates a response or reaction from you. That reaction will create your perception of the Outcomes due to the response to your Actions. A reaction is different from a response. A reaction is taken quickly without any consideration, while a response usually requires some moments to consider the appropriate Action to take. Armed with this information, you can now guide your Outcomes by achieving Desired results from properly planned, prepared responses to be carried out. The tools contained in this book were compiled to provide you with a system that will help you to change your LIFE making it better by helping you to Achieve your Dreams. When I spend some time in careful analysis of my circumstances considering my options to ensure that any decisions made are ideal & come up with a plan of Action, then my Outcomes is likely to be one I am appreciative in the end. It may not be the Outcomes I Desire, but it is ideal & the harder I work toward my goals, the closer I get.

That is my goal in writing this book. I have every intention of LIVING better days, of LIVING a future that I Desire. That intention requires work, consideration & constant effort. I must consider on every occasion what steps to take & whether they are the right decisions & Actions. When I didn't, it would often prove costly. Who am I?

So, just who am I? Why should I bother to offer my advice or guidance to you? What concern is it of mine whether you LIVE a better LIFE or not? I could just use these tools for myself & LIVE a better LIFE for myself, with little care for anyone else.

Better yet, why should you take my advice? Who am I to be telling you how to LIVE your LIFE?

I'm a professional bus driver who once was happy with everything about LIFE. That joy for LIFE was short LIVED & slowly began to dwindle with the demands of the job, not to mention the fact that I was broke which took a heavier toll on me & my household. My LIFE became hectic & I became distraught, unhappy because I wasn't LIVING the LIFE I Desired. Hate began to build up inside of me. I would take things personally, becoming offended because of the difficulties I was faced with daily.

I began to hate my job, hate that I was always broke, hate my professional LIFE & my home LIFE because I hated the way my LIFE had worked out. Things changed in my LIFE thus they began to change in my mind too. My thoughts & my Attitude started to affect not only who I was, but it also had an overlapping effect on those around me.

That Attitude began to bleed into my personality. It changed me, for the worse not better. When things went wrong, I would place that Attitude at the forefront as a defensive mechanism. The statement, "I don't care!" became the dominant expression of my LIFE. At other times I would dismiss people by saying, "Whatever!"

Chapter 7

My Attitude:

I used to say, "I don't care." My boss decided to call me out on that one. He disagreed, stating that I do care. If I didn't, I wouldn't get so upset or become offended when people do certain things, Act a certain way or things don't go my way, as they often will. From that moment I learned that I truly do care & began to embrace that as part of my being.

It turns out I really do care! I care how LIFE affects me, how it affects those closest to me & even those within my circle of influence. I care because their LIVES do affect me. It also bothered me what others do, especially as it affects me & mine. I would take things personally, though I knew better until I heard it spoken to me in such terms, there was little possibility to behave or think any differently.

I became aware of my Attitude towards others & that allowed me to change my thinking. I have learned that my Attitude is more important to my success than aptitude. This was the first bit of work I had to Achieve. I had to develop a new Attitude toward LIFE. My LIFE was miserable & I was unhappy because I had a negative Attitude about LIFE itself. Then there was the fact that I blamed everything that happened to me on either the world at large or someone specific who had done me wrong.

At that time in my LIFE I would say things like, "Why do these things always happen to me?" Or "That's just my LIFE." These were among so many negative thoughts that kept me from seeing the real reason that had me LIVING a hard LIFE. I was so blinded by hatred that people even had a hard time convincing me that I possessed such a negative Attitude. I was a good man, but the world is conspiring to keep me down. That was my prevalent thought & looking back now I can see how absurd that was.

I have learned that I must not take things personally. I have learned that each person sees things from their own perspective. This reaction from someone else is not personal to me but to the individual who presents it. When I would get upset or angry over a situation that I witnessed, I was the one taking it personally. When I would stress because I was running late, or someone cut me off in traffic, I was the one who took it personal. When I would tear someone a new one because they had done something that offended me, I was the one taking it personal.

The problem became that I was not the only one this affected. When I would get upset over seemingly small matters, I would carry that Attitude with me for hours afterward & those who met with me would often bear the brunt of my ire. I was getting upset over the way LIFE was treating me, but also things I was witness to that did not concern me, like driving in traffic getting annoyed because someone cut me off, or even when they would just be driving aggressively whether or not it affected me. As soon as I was able to let that practice go, I found myself in a better mental state. People who mattered to me noticed the difference in me almost immediately.

I will say that I did not do this alone. I doubt that I would have been able to recover from this pit of despair on my own. Though people were pointing out these signs to me, I know that I could not have changed who I had become or the way I reacted to people or circumstances. I had to seek the guidance of a professional counsellor. Thankfully I was able to receive help in putting some pieces of myself back together. This was a benefit that was available to me through my employer & I took advantage of it, once I became aware of how I was affecting not only myself but everyone I interacted with.

It is sad to realize now that I had just about chased every person close to me away. I didn't see it until I almost lost the person closest to me, the one person who had vowed to stand by me through good times & bad. It must have gotten truly bad for her to consider whether to stay & fight or just walk away because I obviously didn't want her around anymore.

At this stage of my LIFE I was in such a state that I almost lost my job, my house & my spouse. This was enough to scare me into taking Action to resolve my horrible circumstances that all stemmed from my Attitude.

I have done a lot of work on myself in the past seven years. I have learned that I was dissatisfied with who I was, the LIFE I LIVED. I have learned that these circumstances were because of the position I had placed myself. I had to come to terms with the fact that I was responsible for the Outcomes of my LIFE. 100% Responsible! I was the one who had put myself there. I have learned that I was the only one who could change my Outcomes to make my LIFE better.

"You have a responsibility to maintain your response ability." ~ Brian Tracy

This lesson taught by Brian Tracy opened my eyes a little further. When you grasp this statement & consider how the words apply to your LIFE, you will understand, as I did, that you are not being a responsible person if you cannot control your temper, if you do not control your responses. Almost immediately this one practice changed who I was going to become.

Chapter 8

My Studies:

"When the student is ready, the teacher will appear."
~ Spiritual Philosophy attributed to The Buddha

I have studied from many of the masters of personal development: Tony Robbins, Zig Ziglar, Brian Tracy, Napoleon Hill, Stephen Covey, Robin Sharma & John Maxwell among others, but more locally there is Raymond Aaron, a teacher in the movie; *The Secret.* Raymond Aaron was the teacher of the first seminar I have ever attended. I have been addicted to them ever since. He is also the personal mentor of those who now mentor me personally. I am privileged to get both direct (Seminars) & indirect (Mentees) influence from Raymond Aaron. He has taught those who now teach & influence me. One of the main reasons for my dedication to studies from these powerful people is that they passed on their collected knowledge & wisdom to me.

Mentors are another means of growing exponentially. By seeking out mentors who can aid in my growth directly, I continue to learn. Never stop learning through books, audios & videos, training or collegiate courses & of course through the direct influence of mentors who can guide you on your personal journey.

One of the things Raymond planted in my mind was the notion that there are so many things in LIFE that we concern ourselves with that we would better off if we were not to bother demonstrating concern over.

He placed it in a graph of overlapping circles. One circle showed the things that affect us personally. The other circle was those things that we have control over. The section where the two circles overlap is what may garner some attention. This is where the event or circumstance affect you directly & you may have some control over the Outcomes.

If you consider the events or Outcomes that affect you as the first circle, then the second circle represents the items or circumstances over which you have control. The intersecting sections is the important area that affect you & you have control over the Outcomes. This is where you should bother exerting your efforts, all the rest would be best served if they were removed from your mind. By turning your attention to only the section that affects you & that you have some control over the Outcomes you are limiting your stress level. Your aggravation level is almost eliminated because you are only working on those items that affect you that you can do something about. The diagram shown below demonstrates this principle.

I mentioned my studies; they came in the form of books, webinars, seminars, videos, audios, some training courses & most especially mentors. Any knowledge I could absorb in the realm of personal development now had my full attention. I began to absorb everything I could that would help me become a better person. That was my only goal at the time, to become the person my wife would love again. That required changing the thinking that was going on in my mind.

"You are who you are & what you are because of what goes into your mind."
~ Zig Ziglar

The first book that reignited the passion I had for learning, enough so that I would continue my journey for studies & personal growth, came at a time I needed it most. I was in a severe negative state & I was falling fast. At one of the worst times in my LIFE, I discovered an invaluable book.

That book; *Make Today Count; John Maxwell.*

The wisdom contained in that book helped to change my outlook on LIFE, helped me want to LIVE a Better LIFE. The book allowed me to consider that I was not making today the most important day in my LIFE. I wanted to LIVE it again & it helped me to realize that I was not truly LIVING LIFE. This book gave me a new lease on LIFE. It began to plant in my mind, the possibilities that my LIFE might hold for the future.

This book, which I now hold so dearly led to two other books which held valuable wisdom that every person should read. If you have not read them yet, pick up a copy of these three books:

- *How to Win Friends & Influence People; Dale Carnegie*

- *Think & Grow Rich, Napoleon Hill,* & of course.

- *Make Today Count (or) Today Matters; John Maxwell*

These 3 amazing books when taken together offers lessons that will change anyone's LIFE for the better. These books also lead to other books & lessons.

Everything I have learned in becoming the man I am today suggests that LIFE itself & most importantly that MY LIFE is not about me. It's about all those people who come into my LIFE. All LIFE is about others, the connections we have, the people we meet & the relationships we keep. LIFE is about the interactions we have with those who come into our LIVES.

By making those relationships important & placing great effort on the care or concerns of others, we make our LIVES just that much better. Now I am not suggesting that you take their LIVES into your worried, busy LIFE. We just suggested not to attempt to control those events that do not affect you. But consider that there are other people in your LIFE. Your LIFE can be better if those in it are LIVING better LIVES.

Everything you have done or Achieved in your LIFE thus far was because of others. You would not exist if not for the connection of two special people, you may call them Mom & Dad. Then there are teachers, family, friends & so many others to whom we owe our existence & growth. There are those to whom we owe our LIVES because they offer their livelihood to support us; farmers, producers, packagers of products, service providers, doctors, lawyers, etc. They provide skills & assets that we are not able to provide for ourselves.

You are not alone! You do not have to LIVE your LIFE alone. There are others LIVING the same LIFE you do, working on many of the same things as you. By working with others, we make LIFE easier for ourselves.

As parents our main concern is not for us but for our children. We make sure their every need is taken care of, until they can manage that for themselves. Our children lead easier lives because we work for them. You will learn many lessons because of the work you do for the survival & growth of your children.

When we transfer that same practice to others by seeing to their needs, we can gain a better position in our own LIFE. You have heard the expression, "What comes around, goes around." This can be taken as both a Positive & negative fact. This offers reference to the Law of Attraction which states, "LIKE ATTRACTS LIKE." Therefore, it pays dividends to be Positive rather than negative, be nice rather than mean & have goodness rather than hatred in your heart. To work for others rather than being selfish.

When we care for those who offer value to our LIVES, it ensures that we will receive the Positive benefits of such a relationship. It also offers a means for us to let things go. When we consider this, it bears to mind that if they choose to be negative, hateful or Act in a distasteful manner they will get what is coming to them. They will pay the price for the negativity they display, just as you will benefit from the goodness & positivity you offer to others who cross your path.

"You can have everything in LIFE you want if you just help enough other people get what they want." ~ Zig Ziglar

You see, I am just using you to get what I want.

OK, not really. I am not a selfish being.

Even in my youth, my concern & my efforts were often for my friends more than myself. What were their needs? What could I do for them? How I could I make their LIVES easier? I will say that I was not so enlightened as I am now (I still have far to go). I would become insulted that they did not feel the same or return the favor & offer me the same courtesy. I would find myself getting offended that they did not take care of my needs in many situations.

So, in a way though, I am using you.

I should be using you, as you should be using me. We should be Working Together. We are better & stronger together. United in a common cause, we gain support in trying to Achieve our Dreams. By working together, we can gain the advantage of leveraging each other's talents. When we work together, we can help other improve our circumstances & LIVE a better LIFE. My LIFE has a better opportunity of becoming a success just by helping others Achieve their Dreams, but if they agree to offer the same in return, we are a stronger force when united. Like a rope that is built of strands of string, when we combine them, they create a tool that is strong & offers powerful leverage that has provided tremendous value to the growth of humanity.

Again, "Like attracts like." Refer to the "Golden Rule". Take care of others as they will take care of you. Your LIFE will absolutely improve, not only by helping others but with help from others, from the right people in the right places that make up for areas you may be lacking. Use other people. Let others use you. Build a TEAM (Together Everyone Achieves More) dedicated to your success. Make sure that this is an equal exchange, so you will get taken advantage of. Offer your services, skills & talents as a value exchange. Help others as they would help you. Another word for use is utilize, you are not using each other which sounds negative, but utilizing the resources of others that you do not possess. Utilization of these resources offers greater leverage, making up for the areas you may be lacking to accomplish your own needs & Desires. But be sure to return the favor & allow others to utilize your skills or assets. These relationships should be a give & take, not unilateral transactions.

Some of the lessons I have learned...

- I have learned that working together is better than working alone. We would be better building a World Together, not tearing apart the one we have.

- I have learned to work hard to help those people that matter to me.

- I have learned to demonstrate concern for the Outcomes of others.

- I have learned that we should work to build up others, to LIVE a LIFE of service.

- I have learned that by helping others become better, it is very likely I might become better myself.

Each of us work hard to LIVE the best LIFE we possibly can. But for most of us, it's not a LIFE we LOVE to LIVE. My LIFE has evolved to help others LIVE a LIFE they LOVE. By learning everything I have, in the efforts of my personal growth, LIFE has now allowed me the opportunity to #SHARETHEWISDOM with others, working with others not only for my benefit but for the benefit of others, which helps to make the world just that much better. The benefit others receive, they gain my useful skills or knowledge that may ease their burden while it tends to make my LIFE just that much better for having aided them.

Chapter 9

Why do I care?

I am RJ Horner
I know who I am!
I know where I am going!
I know what I am doing to get there!

I don't say that boastfully, I know who I am. This took a lot of time spent in self-analysis. I have learned that what I gain is in proportion to what I bring. That is what I want to offer each of you through this material; knowledge of self.

You will get in touch with who you are & what you want.

How else can you Achieve your Outcomes if you don't know what those Outcomes may be?

Get to know your inner Desires, your passions, & let's not forget or deny your faults, behaviors & Attitude. Few people spend enough on themselves if it doesn't have immediate satisfaction; hair, nails, gym... I have learned that the greatest satisfaction will come to those who invest in themselves long-term.

There are three pillars that will help you elevate your LIFE to the next level; hold you steady in your search for your Desired Outcomes. You will gain a better position through the implementation of these pillars. If you are yet unaware of them, two of them most of us are familiar with. The third is less accessible to us, but this can be offered through the TEAMs we are looking to help you assemble.

The first two available pillars; A Vision & A Desire to Achieve it. The third is the means to make it happen. If you only ask…the right people!

The missing piece in that success formula is accountability. A business owner is responsible for all the people they employ, but unless you own a business, you may not know where that accountability comes from. This business I am now running is my own venture, my own Dream & now my own reality. I have vision, I have Desire, but because I alone am responsible for it, there is no accountability.

This formula for Success will take you to new heights of success;

Vision + Desire + Accountability

Family is accountable to each other, especially a mother or father, raising children with all the responsibility that carries with it. When working with others, you are held accountable to the other members of the TEAM.

If you have thought yourself previously unaccountable, you must now exert a more serious, concerting effort to accomplish the tasks you are assigned. You owe the people you are working with that much.

When we work together to Achieve our Dreams, whether those Dreams are yours, mine or Dreams we share; We can Achieve them as a TEAM. We are stronger together as a united force. Those Outcomes we Desire have a higher degree of certainty.

No Outcome is ever guaranteed. No matter how hard you try, regardless of all the effort you might exude in trying to make things work out your way, there are obstacles that will still arise. LIFE is like that. You try to make LIFE as easy as it possibly can be, fact is the best you can do is try. Your efforts are not wasted, but they can feel fruitless if you let them.

So why not give up? Why work so hard to have things work out the way you want them to if you are likely to fail most of the time? Consider the alternative…

You give up, stop fighting, or at least go with the flow. Let LIFE happen as it will. You just go about your days doing what you must, ignoring all the things that happen to you, passing it off as, "That's just the way things are, nothing I can do about it." Under those terms LIFE will rarely go as you want it to go.

I often picture LIFE as a River…

Let's take trip down that River of LIFE.

You go with the flow, just drifting along at a slow, peaceful pace. But every river has a rocky bottom. That drag could cause some issues. The pace can change at any moment. It can slow or pick up, moving you quickly through the rapids. As it gets faster, you are bound to get a few bumps & bruises.

Then the unsightly happens, you may not see the waterfall ahead, where there are limited choices available. You can go over, falling fast or choose to jump ship, where you either sink or swim. Those along for the ride must also make the same choice, whether they should jump ship & swim for safety or stay with you, where it is likely that the entire ship will go overboard.

If going with the flow is the decision you make, then you can forever forget that Dream of achieving anything substantial in your LIFE. Don't get me wrong, you just might. It is possible that your blissful ignorance might lead you to a LIFE of success & happiness unimaginable to some. There is also the chance that your LIFE will be filled with difficulties & strife, but that brings its own concerns & the ones that we are trying to avoid.

If leaving LIFE to chance is the decision you make, you can do nothing to improve it. By leaving LIFE to chance, you can never be involved in the Outcomes of your LIFE. You have little influence in the Outcomes. You must not complain about how bad things are for you & you are likely to get frustrated when LIFE doesn't work out the way you want.

If you are the type to just let it all go or you make that decision, then you must forever forfeit the right to the thoughts, feelings & emotions associated with any unsatisfactory Outcomes. You may allow yourself to experience the joys, but you cannot complain, condemn or despair because of your circumstances. You have made your choice, even if that was to not make one. You must LIVE with whatever circumstances arise in your LIFE. You have little choice but to accept the unwanted Outcomes.

You may note that Acceptance is one of the tools offered here. That Acceptance does not mean that you should forget about or ignore the bad things that happen, or not to do anything more than wish for a better tomorrow, but to endure until a better time to Act might arise. The choice to LIVE LIFE belongs to you. Therefore, the power to Build a LIFE you LOVE to LIVE lies solely in your hands.

Make that decision! Doing so can take your LIFE to an unimaginable level that you would forfeit the right to when you let LIFE work itself out as it may. Make the conscious decision to improve your LIFE & your circumstances. By taking LIFE into your own hands you begin to make it better. Just by the simple Act of a decision, offers you a conscious effort to make your LIFE all that you might want it to be. Let it be, or Let it be yours. The choice is yours!

Chapter 10

LIVING Your LIFE:

"Some people say, LIVE & Let LIVE, but if this ever-changing world in which we LIVE in makes you give in & cry...Say, LIVE & Let Die!" ~ Paul McCartney, The Beatles

What you find in the pages of this book are tools that will help you LIVE & Let LIVE, help you let go of the strife & pain that arise in each our LIVES, on any given day of LIFE. You will find a step-by-step process that will walk you towards an Outcomes that has a higher chance of satisfaction. There are no guarantees that the effort will work out to your favor, but with the process offered in these pages, you have a technique that can lead you closer to any Outcomes you Desire.

If you have experienced strife up to date & let's face it, who hasn't, it is time now to open your mind to the possibility of another way of LIFE. Despite what I have said to the contrary, I can make one guarantee. I can absolutely guarantee that you will still experience hard times. But things that matter are hard.

If something is worth it to you, then it is worth working through. It is worth LIVING.

Consider that & apply it to your current position & the Dreams you Desire using the steps provided. Your LIFE will work out better. You can change your ways because you can change your thinking. Using these tools WILL make your LIFE easier, better than you ever imagined. Your thought process will be altered as you become practiced at using this tool.

Though this does work well as a step process, there is no need to perform them in order. There are several tools here that if utilized that can make every Outcomes much easier. Some of these steps will also be easy to use, others require more thought & in-depth analysis.

As you become better practiced at them, you may not need to write down or track through most of these steps. In the beginning, use them in order as often as possible to get in the habit. If you are looking for a Desired Outcomes or just want to get better at decision making, you should become familiar with utilizing these steps. Though It is not a requirement, you can handle any situation your own way, but with the consideration & utilization of these steps you can Achieve the Outcomes you want.

Take heed of the words you will read in the pages ahead. This tool really is a miracle. It was provided to me as if by divinity. It comes from no other source that I can verify, except as it was compiled from the years of study I have made in the field of personal development. It was pieced together as much from the ether as from all the study I have taken upon myself to undertake in my own growth & development.

The first two concepts in Personal Development, change & growth are absolute facts for ALL LIFE!

- Change is inevitable! Every molecule is continually circulating to accommodate the movement of ALL LIFE.

- Every living sentient being must also continue to grow & evolve!

These are facts you must be aware of. You cannot ignore them. These facts are part of those Universal Laws I value so much.

With all likelihood, it is entirely possible that these steps came about as a result of that study of those Universal Laws. By whatever means this information came to me, they are vital tools that have aided my LIFE in its growth to the level it has thus far. It has removed the chance of luck or hope & all but ensured that I will have a Positive Outcomes.

You have read this far. By now I have convinced you that the information contained in the pages ahead will help you LIVE a Better LIFE!

Learn these steps; write them down somewhere that you may refer to them in times of need. They are an invaluable resource for Your LIFE! What you will find moving forward is that you have the power in your hands & in your mind to make your LIFE all you want it to be. Like LIFE, you will not experience instant change, but this 8-step process, plus a couple of special bonus tools contained within, WILL help you grow & Achieve the Outcomes you Desire.

With each of these steps, I will refer to their definition first, so that you understand what is being described. Knowing what is described, you will be able to consider how it applies, not only to the terms of reference but also to your unique situation.

This report was compiled to ensure that each of us might have the tool that has helped me endure LIFE. You too can grow your confidence & develop a pride that previously could not have been allowed in my LIFE, just a few short years ago. Unfortunately, I still get it wrong on occasion, those are the times that I shoot from the hip. Whenever I Act without consideration for the future & the results I want to Achieve, or without taking the time to consider my options or the Outcomes I Desire.

I have proven to myself on countless occasions, that when I take the time to consider my position & implement at least some of the steps listed within, LIFE was easier. I am confident in saying that if you come to understand & employ these steps, you too will LIVE a Better LIFE. Perhaps you might even Build a LIFE You LOVE to LIVE!

Here are those 10 steps.

- **Attitude**
- **Awareness**
- **Acceptance**
- **Acquiesce**
- **Ascertain**
- **Assess**
- **Analyze**

- o **Adjudicate**
- o **Action**
- o **Ask**

For each of the steps we will first look at the definition. All definitions are taken from MS Office; Smart Lookup feature. The information is provided by **Oxford Dictionaries; Oxford University Press**.

Even though they are listed below, I suggest you keep reading to truly understand the steps & how to implement them. Deep dive into the content & become familiar with these steps. They were created to help all of us Achieve our Desired Outcomes.

You cannot combat anything if you are unaware of just what you are up against. Let's starts looking at the 10 Steps to Achieve any Outcomes You Desire! As I mentioned, Here I offer you two bonus A's. I discovered one special word as I was writing this book. This one has been documented throughout the book. It has been written down in these pages so often that it should be implanted in your mind, so deeply in fact that it has now entered your subconscious.

This A is so vital to the sequence of steps that they do not operate the same without this one. If you do not utilize this ALL IMPORTANT 'A', then you WILL NOT Achieve the Outcomes you so Desire. This is the one I discovered throughout my writing

No, it is not Achievement, though that one is in this book often, especially as that is what this book is all about, like the key topic.

If you think back, you will realize that you know this, because it was mentioned in just about every chapter. Your Outcomes would have been very different if you didn't heed this word already.

Put the *10 Steps to Achieve any Outcome you Desire* to work for you…

Chapter 11

Step 1: Attitude

i. a settled way of thinking or feeling about someone or something, typically one that is reflected in a person's behavior

"The only disability in life is a bad Attitude." Scott Hamilton

One of the first things you must overcome if you wish to Achieve anything in your life is your Attitude.

That word that is so vital it appears at the beginning & the end of our process…ATTITUDE. It comes as a general reminder that Attitude, especially a Positive Attitude is so important to our success that we will not Achieve the same results without it.

"Your mental Attitude attracts to you everything that makes you what you are." ~ Napoleon Hill

Without a Positive Attitude you are likely to make negative decisions or Actions. With the entire point of growing & becoming better, you are trying to change things from a negative to a Positive. Your Attitude is the starting point of everything you are trying to Achieve.

You want your LIFE to become better. You are trying to Achieve a Positive Outcomes.

If you have a Positive Attitude from the start, then you have that advantage before you started. A Positive Attitude whenever you can maintain it, can be a game-changer. Every moment of your LIFE could be happy, joyful & satisfactory with a Positive Attitude. If you do not possess that Attitude at this stage, start with that. Work on your Attitude, then begin this work again. I promise that you will Achieve satisfactory Outcomes for most instances you encounter.

I learned early on that my Attitude was my problem. It was what was causing family breakdown. It was what was causing those around me to dwindle as they run & hide at first sight of me. It was what was keeping me from enjoying people & moments. There are times to enjoy, we sometimes forget that, with our petty wants & needs…especially when those needs are not met.

It was that my Attitude was always so negative that the negative was all I saw, all I received more of because that was the frequency I was on. I LIVED & breathed negativity for years…for what? Because I didn't pay attention to what was going on around me. Furthermore, if anyone told me I was being negative in any way; angry, upset, crabby irritable, bitchy, then I would snap. LOSE IT!

I was my own worst enemy because my Attitude said a lot before my mouth even opened. My body language, my facial expression, even my stature represented my irate mood. "You better not cross me."; "I dare you to cross me!"; "Find a way to cross me." Although cross is a much better term then the words I would have used.

I learned that if I changed my Attitude to an Attitude with a Positive frequency then I would begin to revolve on that frequency. If was to give that frequency, it would bounce off others & return to me. When I learned this principle, I had nothing to lose, but why not try it. I put this practice to work & quicker than you would think at that time, I was starting to receive Positive returns.

I don't want to assume anything, but it seems that if you are trying to look for better Outcomes in your LIFE then you would want them to be Positive ones. To accomplish Positive Outcomes, you must go into these steps with a Positive Attitude. A negative Attitude just won't due.

When you find yourself in a charged moment, things aren't going as planned, there are things you can do to relieve it.

1. You could sing show-tunes…These are a few of my favorite things…

- Laugh or sneer if you want, but you can't be sad or angry & Julie Andrews has soothed my mood on more than one occasion.

- I choose the song above because it helps to think of things you enjoy

- Sing something, anything that makes you happy.

- Sing Metallica if it brings you joy.

2. Count to 10, of course.

- We knock this one sometimes, but it really helps. Chuck your Pride & consciously count to ten.
- Breathe, take it easy. Practice breathing techniques if you can, there are many articles & books on the subject.
- In – Out, In – Out.

3. Just walk away! When you find yourself upset...;

- Walk away:
- Leave them wondering rather than leave them without a doubt.

The Law of Attraction states that "Like attracts Like!" That means that whatever vibrations or energy you put forth you will receive in kind. You will receive whatever you put out into the Universe as if in a mirror reflection.

This suggests that you must first adjust your Attitude to become more Positive. The Gurus of Personal Development will tell you that if you are not receiving the blessings you Desire, then you are not doing enough in this area. You are not Positive enough. You are still harboring some thoughts that are negative in nature.

Thoughts like, "I'm not good enough" or

"When are good things going to happen to me?" or even,

"This is just my LIFE!"

"The world is against me."

If you have not gotten complete control over your Attitude, fear not, it comes with practice & time. But decide to emit only Positive energy, so that you may receive only Positive energy in return.

Allow only positivity into your LIFE as well. Remove negative influences like the NEWS! This is the most-evil for your mind. Negative shows, the 1st to come to mind is *King of Queens,* Doug is forever trying to pull one over on Carrie. Trying to outsmart her or get out from under her control. Negative people, while this one is more difficult, you must recognize when a person only brings negativity to the relationship. Any time this is the case, it is a travesty that must be repaired.

These thoughts all bear negative energy that can keep your Positive energy from giving you what you want.

If you reflect negative energy or thoughts, then you will receive negativity in return, but if your thoughts are all Positive then the Universe cannot help but offer you more Positive vibrations, thus the Outcomes you have will tend to be Positive. Practice altering your behavior, thoughts & Attitude now. You will need to retain that positivity throughout the remainder of these steps. Especially as you move to the next step.

Chapter 12

Step 2: Awareness:

     i. Knowledge or perception of a situation or fact

    ii. Concern about and well-informed interest in any situation or development.

To be aware of something means you know about it, you show concern for it. You know it exists, whether you know its purpose or not. That means you pay it the attention it deserves. If anything appears in your LIFE, whether good or bad, you only know about it once you pay attention to it.

The masters of Personal Development say that what you focus on expands & this also has a reference to the Law of Attraction, where like attracts like. If what you focus on expands & like attracts like, then if you think, talk or Act negative…negative is what you will receive. If you remain negative & emit negative vibrations, then you will remain negative because that is what you are focusing on.

On the opposite end, we are trying to turn your LIFE in a more Positive direction. If you send out good vibrations, LIVE & breathe Positive energy, then you can only receive more of that Positive energy in return. Good things come to good people…most of the time.

You should also be aware if you are in a constant negative vibrational state, so you may change your state.

We often do not notice our state of being, how negative our LIFE is becoming, or even how we are behaving until we are hit hard by LIFE. Often, we must hit rock bottom before we can climb out of the depths that we find ourselves in. Even before we get to this state there are signs that LIFE is headed in a negative direction. Those signs, we might call issues or problems that we experience in our day-to-day LIVING.

As with any negative occurrence or Outcomes, you might call them a challenge, problem or concern. As with any of these issues you MUST be aware of the circumstances. If you are unaware, how can you understand your situation or your current state? If you become aware of any circumstance, you can influence the Outcomes. You must be thoroughly aware of your immediate circumstance or current position in LIFE in order to change it. You must be aware of the predicament you are in, so that you may alter this.

At this stage I want to introduce you to CBT; Cognitive Behavioral Therapy. It was another tool delivered to me when I needed it most. This was offered as a technique through the counselling I received in the efforts to recover my sanity, change my behavior & dissolve my negative Attitude.

I don't propose to be a master of this technique. I just know that it worked for me, when I needed my eyes opened into my soul; who I was, how I was behaving. This was the main method to alter that behavior. Cognitive Behavioral Therapy is the technique that offered me a chance at removing the negativity & hatred I had begun to possess, or rather it began to possess me. It allowed me to start moving toward becoming a better, happier man.

By being aware of your behaviors, you can alter them, & by implementing CBT, you have a major tool to changing your LIFE for the better.

If you think you might be experiencing negativity or have been often told that you possess a bad habit or negative trait. YOU don't believe you do, but you have heard people tell you often enough, so just for a moment, amuse us.

Take some time to understand this process because it will help you, with any behavior you wish to eradicate. Begin by taking notes; when you have a thought, a notion, a bad habit or negative moment, chart how that thought affected you (made you feel, think, Act), what could you have done differently to receive a Positive Outcomes.

Work this out on a spreadsheet…

Thought/Act	Reaction	Response

This spreadsheet that can be placed in any notebook. Take a page or a spreadsheet on your CPU. You want to document all negative thoughts or emotions you have or the Actions you take. Then the reaction you had as a result of that thought or Action. Finally, you want to consider a new, more appropriate response for that thought or Act.

You won't get this right off the bat, but it will take practice in getting this habit forming, LIFE altering technique. With practice, you will eventually change your thinking with little effort, without a spreadsheet, you will be able to make appropriate responses that lead to your Desired Outcomes more often rather than not. By doing this, you can begin working toward a more Positive state & better Outcomes. When you become aware of something, you can change it. The basic practice of monitoring your thoughts & behaviors will allow you to alter those behaviors over time. With this practice, over time you can do this automatically.

Without taking the effort, you cannot realize just how negative you are becoming, or just how bad your circumstances are. When you start paying attention to the thoughts & behaviors you are having, you have the potential to change them for the better, or worse.

But why would you want to become worse? The entire point of Personal Development is to become better. So, if you are using this tool, if you picked up a copy of this book, the likelihood is that you are working on becoming better. You can improve circumstances & Build a Better LIFE. That is another main purpose of all LIFE, to continually improve & become better.

To make any progress or change your state, that current state MUST be brought to the forefront of your Awareness through your attention to it. You MUST become aware of what is truly going on. You MUST be aware of what LIFE is bringing to you or what is currently going on in your LIFE, where you want to go in LIFE...Dream Big...& truly WANT to go there. Possess the Desire, then go make it happen. You want to become aware of your current circumstances, combine that with the Desires you have. You want to know where you want to go in LIFE & the things you want to Achieve. Knowing where you are & what you want, you can make progression, going toward your Dreams rather than further away. This is the simplest formula for achieving your Desired Outcomes.

Become aware of where you are, know where you want to go, now go there.

As Larry the Cable Guy says; "Git 'er Done!" Know what you want & go get it.

There are rules of course...ones of etiquette, survival, humanity, humility & more. The characteristics of becoming a better human being are the guiding factors in getting what you want. Work on who you are, then you can work on who you want to be. If you want to be better at anything then you must build your character first.

Start with, becoming aware of who you are now.
- What are your values?
- What are your hopes, Desires, Dreams & aspirations?

- o No matter how trivial; No matter how extravagant…
- o Allow your hopes to become intentions
- o DREAM BIG!
- Where do you want to go?
- What do you want to do?
- What would you like to Achieve?

WRITE IT DOWN!

To put this in perspective, use this method taught by Jim Rohn…

- o Write down all YOUR Dreams & Desires.
- o Everything your mind can Dream or imagine
- o List at least 50! (Jack Canfield & Mark Victor Hansen suggest 101)
  - Prof., personal, study,
    - Education or training
  - Travels, vacation spots; Egypt, Caribbean Cruise
  - Home, Mortgage Free, Cottage/Vacation Home
  - Shopping, Dress, Shoes, etc.
  - Car(s)… Paid Cash?
  - Wishes you could have, do, be?
- o DREAM BIG. BE LOFTY.
- How do you want to LIVE LIFE? Really LIVE LIFE?
  - o Think about your Dream 50 above.
  - o Think about your ideal LIFE.

- o Describe what YOUR LIFE looks like.
- When do you want to Achieve them?
  - o Label your Dream 50 according to when you could possibly Achieve them.
  - o Mark; 1, 2, 5, 10 or 20, (The timeline in years that it would take you Achieve these goals.)

This Dream 50 exercise helps put your LIFE in perspective. Doing this determines your direction in LIFE. You now know what you want, where you want to go & how soon you want to Achieve them? Those things marked 1, consider which one or two things are attainable right now. Make sure they are ones you would be pleased to complete. Create a plan for their attainment. Do the same thing with the 2 year marked items, 5 Years & so on.

There are other techniques you can use. Vision exercises that you can do to picture your LIFE, as you want it to go.

This next one I call the Bonsai method…

How many of you remember the original Karate Kid movie series? In one of the movies, the Bonsai method was described briefly by Daniel's Karate Teacher. Mr. Miagi says when teaching Danielsan about the Bonsai tree,

- o "Close Eyes.
- o See picture?
- o Open Eyes.

o Make like picture!"

That Bonsai is your DREAM!

"MAKE LIKE PICTURE!"

That Dream becomes your Vision of what you want. This described technique is essentially the meditation method. Meditate on the vision of your Dreams, your future or anything you truly want. By understanding what you want, you have opened yourself to the possibility that you might obtain it.

How can you get there ASAP? We all get hung up on how to make that Dream happen…now? We get so upset that we cannot have that Dream now, not believing that we must work for that Dream to make it happen.

That is where the Dream 50 comes into play. By the time you are finished with these steps, you will have Achieved what you want.

You must do the work. You have the Dream, but you must possess the will to make it happen. If you do, these steps will be a no-brainer.

Take a chance, make it happen, just like the vision you imagine.

When is the best time to plant a tree? 20 Years ago!

When is the second-best time? Yesterday! Yesterday is the best time, but today is better than never because tomorrow never comes.

Make your Hopes & Dreams become intentional. Put a Plan together for how you can make it happen, at the earliest possible opportunity.

I saw these words just about the time I was writing this…It's ok to miss a deadline, not an opportunity! Decide what you want, as soon as you can, so you may begin today, take advantage of those opportunities that are in line with your Dreams as they are presented to you.

First & foremost you MUST become aware of YOU!

The REAL YOU!

Who are you? Get in touch with yourself. Where are you now? What are your current circumstances?

Then determine just what it is you want & how to get you there.

Now that you know what you want, we can move on to the next step in our progression toward the Outcomes.

The next step is where you put yourself in alignment for the upcoming potential growth. You have begun to understand who you are & what you want out of LIFE. But now is where the deep work begins. This step can derail you if you let it. You will get deep within yourself, you will address your psyche, cutting to the deep of who you are.

I prepare you for that, so that you won't give up. It will get difficult to look deep into yourself this way. Be prepared for what is to come.

I am about to ask you to accept who you are & why you are here.

Why are in this position you find yourself. It may sound simple at this stage, but nobody really likes taking a deep look into their being.

Chapter 13

Step 3: Acceptance –

    i. The Action of consenting to receive or undertake something offered

    ii. Agreement with or belief in an idea, opinion, or explanation

    iii. Willingness to tolerate a difficult or unpleasant situation.

You are going to accept the above conditions before moving on from this stage. You will consent to receive feedback & analysis of your existence. You will know that your position was possible to avoid & is reversible. You will tolerate your position…NO LONGER!

Before we begin our next topic, I ask that you go back to the notes you made during the Awareness stage. Look at them & read them deeply. Understand that these are your DREAMS…your true wants & Desires.

Why shouldn't you have them? Its ok to want a good life for you & yours, right?

By now you have come to know some things about yourself & the direction you Desire for your LIFE. You have questioned who you are as a person & what type of person you want to be? You should know who you are & where you want to be, or have a more certain idea anyway & a new direction to head in. Maybe you will even have a renewed sense of purpose.

Let's not be too hasty & jump into anything. We cannot trust that far ahead yet. That's ok, let's take this slow. You'll get the hang of it...especially once you learn you can adjust to this River of LIFE along the way, jibing & tacking to the wind & the troubled waters ahead, until those waters aren't so rough anymore.

Next, we begin the real work. We are about to begin the groundwork, building a foundation that you can trust because it is based upon honest forgiveness & humility. The steps in this book are for anyone seeking honest guidance, focus in building lasting character; a Confident Character.

Taking a closer look at the last chapter assignments. You asked some serious questions to find out who you are. Question who you want to be & where you want to be? That is what this is all about.

WHAT THE F' DO YOU WANT?!?

& WHY THE F' AREN'T YOU THERE?!?

WHY THE F' DON'T YOU HAVE THEM?!?

Because you can't! You don't know how! Not by yourself anyway! A man who taught me so much put it best with a quote from one of his Mentors.

"If you're not rich & successful, it's because there is something you don't know!" ~ T Harv Eker

That is another thing to be aware of…be aware of what you don't know, so you may learn it.

If you have not Achieved all you wish, then there is still more you need to learn. You don't have to do it all now & you most certainly don't need to do it alone. There are others in similar stages of life that require more information or aid. Working together we can begin to grow stronger. One day, one moment, one trial at a time.

This is best done with a community behind you, or at least some support. Support & Guidance are what is needed to move forward. You must accept that you do not know it all, you do not have all the skills, knowledge or assets to move forward. By combining your resources & knowledge with that of others you stand a better chance of satisfactory growth.

But before you accept that, you must first come to accept your situation; your current status, your inability to grow further, your lack of knowledge, skills or assets. Most of all, you must accept that you put yourself there. Through the decisions you made & the Actions you took, or a lack of Action if that be the case, you have allowed yourself into this situation.

You must realize that you have what you have or do not have what you do not have because you have brought that about. If you don't have enough, it's because you have not done the right things or done enough to have them. You have made your LIFE what you want to make it.

I have always believed that LIFE is what you make it. I just never realized the implication of that statement early enough.

LIFE is what you make it! You have not learned my story, that is for another time & place. That is difficult to tell, at least here in this forum. I have believed this principle all my LIFE, but I have not made it what I want it to. I also thought that LIFE has placed me where I didn't want to find myself, lost & confounded. I could also not move forward until I accepted one absolute fact. I put myself there.

I am 100% responsible for my LIFE. The Choices I made & the decisions I was faced with are what brought me to my place here & now.

By accepting that YOU ALONE are wholly responsible for your current circumstances, you have given yourself peace of mind. You have found a platform from which to stand that offers you stability & certainty.

By taking ownership of your LIFE, you gain footholds towards taking back control of your future. Knowing who you are, where you want to go & what you intend to do to get there allows for an easier journey, a feasible journey. A journey that is not only possible, but now probable as the Outcomes seems likelier.

We have established that you have Dreams & Desires that you have not Achieved. There are things left unfulfilled that you want.

- You have become aware that you want things & you do not have them, yet.

- You must now accept that those things you want are yours to obtain, if you want them.

- Accept that you can Achieve your Dreams, but if you do nothing to move forward, then you will forever have wishes & Desires that will continue to be unrealized. You will always be left wanting

- Accept that all you want in LIFE will never happen unless you Act out on your Desires

- Accept that your LIFE will forever be unsatisfying unless you take steps to Achieve your Dreams.

- Accept that YOU are the reason you have not Achieved those Dreams to date.

- Accept that you are the only one who can change your circumstances.

Moving toward your goals requires some effort, it requires a plan to get what you want or where you want to be. Any journey requires a map & compass if you want to stay on track & find your way, lest you become lost.

Once you accept what you want to Achieve & that you do not have it because you have placed yourself in this predicament you are in.

Accept that what you want is yours to Achieve & if you don't move towards your Dreams & take what you want, no one will.

Now that you have accepted your circumstances as your own. If you can accept that you are 100% responsible for the Outcomes you have Achieved so far. You accept that you have Dreams unfulfilled & you want more. You probably have a good deal of the direction you want your LIFE to take but without that map, you will forever be lost. Acceptance allows you to move forward with a higher degree of certainty. You can now make progress toward achieving your Desired Outcomes.

If you truly have accepted your position in LIFE, you would find your way forward way enough. But Acceptance is not enough in itself, there is more to the puzzle. This next part requires deep commitment. You must give in to the facts that have presented themselves.

Chapter 14

Step 4: Acquiesce -

    i. To accept something reluctantly but without protest.

    ii. to accept, comply, or submit tacitly or passively — often used with *in* or *to*

This stage is one that still troubles me. I try to just get by or just get along, yet there are things in my LIFE or moments that still present issues for me, like anyone else might, or mine might be worse… Wanting to make things better and making them better are hard to align. I am aware of these moments & that I don't respond well, on occasion.

"You have a responsibility to maintain your response ability." ~ Brian Tracy

I accept that my response ability in the moments are 100% my responsibility. I accept that I fail in that responsibility.

Your wants will come to you, if you want them & you are willing to work for them, but you cannot force them into your hand. You have taken great pains to find out just what you want, where you want to go & the things you want to Achieve.

If you want LIFE to be fair to you, then you must detach yourself from the Outcomes. I know, you want this to happen, but forcing it only makes it that much more difficult to obtain. You want it so bad that you can almost taste it, but you are trying too hard, wanting it too badly.

If you truly Desire something. If you want it so bad it hurts…the only Outcomes you will get are issues. You are trying to force something that is out of your control.

To gain control, you must lose control! **WOW!**

This statement must surely have come from the ether, passed on to me from the Universe, or perhaps I heard it somewhere before, not only is this fitting, but a truly powerful fact that represents the only path out of the darkness. I may have known this to be true, but that kind of wisdom makes me believe in some higher source of consciousness.

I am not a believer in religion. I distrust religious affiliations. I once called myself an atheist, then slowly became an agnostic, that is the path of my growth. Yet there is also powerful wisdom in the phrase, "Let go & let God!" These words are not just a mantra for religious fanatics. They are used to denote the practice of letting go of the Outcomes you Desire. If you let go of that Outcomes, the chances it will come to you become greater.

Why?

The Law of Attraction is once again the practice that makes it possible. We mentioned that the Law of Attraction states that Like attracts Like. Other laws that apply here, the law of rhythm. This is the pendulum effect. Everything goes through cycles. Good times may become bad, just as bad times must eventually turn toward goodness.

You must remove the negativity & bad vibrations that surround you. Dwelling on the things you do not have is allowing negativity to fester in your mind. Whatever troubles you find ailing you are a direct result of the feelings, thoughts & Actions you have harbored up until this point. Whatever troubles you, the issues you have or the harsh feelings & thoughts you bear may be what is holding you back. By letting go of those thoughts & feelings, you allow the goodness & positivity into your LIFE! You allow for the possibility of better Outcomes by removing the blockage of negativity.

"That's easier said than done!"

I know. But think of it this way…that statement is also a negative one that blocks you from getting any further. You may have a hundred more just like it. Here is some wise advice from someone that we all know & LOVE:

"You have to forgive them! Not for them, but for yourself." ~ Madea

Move on. Let it go. Things become easier & LIFE goes a lot smoother if only you can see your way to forgive & forget. Forgive what bothers you. Forgive the fact that you want things & you are not getting what you want. Forgive all the negativity, bad feelings, regret & the thoughts of lacking that keep you grounded in place.

You may not be able to forget, but forgiveness is different. Just accept that it is…it exists, whether you like it or not. If you accept that the thoughts are there & there is nothing you can do about them, but that you can exist without them.

By removing any thoughts or feelings that hold you back, you can make some progression toward the new light that awaits you. You will now be able to enjoy some of the peace & satisfaction that was previously unavailable to you. You can move forward with peace of mind, knowing that the pendulum will start moving in the other direction & LIFE will become easier to manage.

Take some time in meditation on the thoughts you hold & the Attitude you possess, the behaviors & Actions you take. Make sure they are in line with your intentions. Better yet, make sure those intentions are pure. Make sure that what comes from your heart & mind are Positive & filled with good intentions. If they are, the pendulum will start swinging your way.

If you have given serious consideration to this step than perhaps you are ready…

Let go & let God & be ready to allow the Universe to take you further than you ever thought possible before. Acquiescing requires something that a non-secular man, like me might have trouble with. As I mentioned this one still bears some difficulty, though I have been practicing the techniques in this book. For you it may be easier, again they all become easier with practice.

Practice does not make perfect, nothing you do will ever be perfect, but it will become permanent the more you practice. Use these steps as often as you can, on whatever Outcomes you Desire to Achieve & you will gain some strides toward the LIFE you want to LIVE. You stand a great chance of achieving most of the Outcomes you want. You may also find through later steps that the Outcomes you get is not the one you wanted in the first place.

You now have a good understanding of your position in LIFE. You have considered what you want both for your LIFE & what you want to Achieve right now, so let's take a further look at whether what you are seeking is really what you want.

Chapter 15

Step 5: Ascertain -

Definition of *ascertain*
transitive verb

        i.   to find out or learn with certainty; *ascertain* the truth;

        ii.   *archaic* **:** to make <u>certain,</u> exact, or precise

This is an easy one. Don't jump to any conclusions or make assumptions. If you operate with facts, you gain an advantage in removing some negativity up front.

Better days await because of the firewall you put up. You are now placing a barrier between you & subjectification because you are looking a little deeper into the information you are receiving. Before you go making assumptions, get the facts.

Go the source if possible. If you have been provided information by someone make sure it is a direct source. If you are told this by someone else, ask the person it pertains to directly. You do not want second-hand information.

Seek out further research on the internet or other available resources; library, encyclopedia or other people for factual supporting information. Again, though you should seek out the original source, a witness can prove to be reliable.

Like an office, or a detective, you will want to obtain any eye-witness testimony that may be available. Be sure to understand that this source is not direct & may not be truly reliable. It is also possible that this source may not have all the information, they may have made their own assumptions for the missing pieces, added their own opinions, or they may be biased against the potential perpetrator. Be sure to seek out reliable sources or verify if this information & the source is truthful.

Don't believe everything you hear, see or read. Your source may have false information; they may have seen & not heard, or even heard but not seen.
Sometimes the information they receive may be hearsay or gossip, that they have taken for facts. They may also not know the thought process behind the actions taken or not taken.

When you use an alternate source as a reference, know that you are not getting facts, the information may be untrue or misleading. It may be seen from a different angle or far away. It may not be reliable or pertinent to the case at hand. The information may be taken out of context. Getting all the information will help prepare you for moving forward.

Use your experience & judgement to discern if you are getting the right information from the right source for the right reason.

Attain all the facts available. Once you have reliable information, you can make an informed decision. A decision based upon facts & less conjecture will allow for more certainty in the outcomes you desire.

Once you have those facts, you want to take a deep, intense look at what you have & where you stand. It is time for deep structured analysis.

Chapter 16

Step 6: Analyze -

  i. To separate into constituent parts or elements;
      determine the elements or essential features of:

  ii. To examine critically, to bring out the essential
      elements or give the essence:

  iii. To examine carefully and in detail to identify causes,
       key factors, possible results, etc.

  iv. To subject to mathematical, chemical, grammatical,
      etc.

  v. To psychoanalyze.

It is time to look more closely at the data you have obtained…

Now, you have a fair Assessment of your circumstances, it is time to look at what that data means. This is where the hard work comes in. After this step, LIFE will get easier. OK, it's not that grand yet, but you will be much closer to the Outcomes you Desire.

If you have not put it all down on paper, now is the time to do just that. We will now take a deeper look at your position & determine our possible or probable Outcomes. The Outcomes you anticipate may not be the one you will choose after you finish this step. We want this stage to be a deeper look at what circumstances are possible, so that you may come up with a plan for moving forward.

This is the time to get our information organized. If you set about it the right way then you have a picture in your mind of what you might do to make that move, but before you do, you want to be certain that the Actions you take will be correct, at least sufficient. A fuller, deeper examination of the data is required.

Now if this were the corporate world there would be studies performed, teams assembled & detailed reports filed. Those reports would form the basis of analysis. We don't have to spend thousands of dollars or untold man-hours to calculate this, but if you are at all familiar with the corporate world, then you may have heard the term SWOT.

No, not SWAT, though the analysis is similar & they are responsible for special tactics, which is the T in SWOT.

SWOT analysis is a strategy technique that allows you to understand your position based on not only the data you previously compiled but the strategy to lay it out in a pattern that gives you a better picture. It's like a detailed movie trailer of coming events. Once you complete this step, you will have a better understanding of your position.

This is what SWOT is. Getting a detailed analysis of your situation so that you have a clear, thorough understanding. It's a brainstorming session.

As a brainstorming session, you would best be suited to gain the experience of other people in the completion of this step, the more minds the better. Get everything out in the open, on a whiteboard, blackboard or a piece of paper. Write down everything you can think of.

Divide the section of writing tablet into four quarters;

Place an 'S' in the top left corner; 'W' in the Top right corner; 'O' in the bottom Left corner & place a 'T' in the Bottom right. This gives you the framework to Analyze the data you have compiled. The diagram below shows the technique.

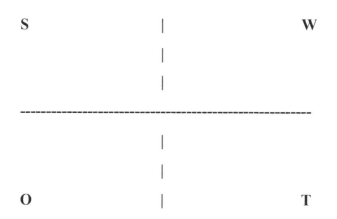

SWOT stands for:

- **Strengths**
- **Weaknesses**
- **Opportunities**
- **Tactics**

Strengths –

- What is it about your current position that gives you strength?
- What gives you power to take specific Action?

- If you take said Action, what position of strength will that offer?
- What assets do you have?
- What resources do you have?
- What connections do you have? Are they unique or special to you & your idea?

Weaknesses –

- What is it about your current position that leaves you weak or vulnerable?
- Are there any holes that put you in a bad position?
- What about your current circumstances take you further back rather than further forward?
- If you took any Action, what weaknesses would that offer to your position?
- What do not have?
- What do you need to acquire?

Opportunities –

- Look at the possibilities…Strengths & Weaknesses
- What steps or Action could you take?
- What opportunities exist that will allow for better positioning or Outcomes.
- Who can you connect to that would help benefit or add value to your idea?
- How can you position yourself that would benefit your idea? List everything you can think of…

Tactics –

- You have enough information to carry out a successful assignment or task.
- Come up with a plan of Action
- Come up with possible tactics or plan of attack

- Piece together a strategy based on possible tactics

These will ultimately become your decision-making choices. If you were to take any Action, what opportunities would that present. You have thoroughly looked at all the information. You have a clearer picture of what Action to take. Make an Actual decision & move forward with certainty.

The Outcomes may be more certain at this point, but nothing is definite yet. You have Assessed your position. This is where you find your path forward based on the SWO' you have compiled.

You have done all you can do, considered all the options. It is all documented, written down in front of you. You can take decisive Action toward the ideal Outcomes you Desire. Now that it is all down in Black & White, you can have a look at the snapshot you have created.

Chapter 17

Step 7: Assess

> i. To evaluate or estimate the nature, ability or quality of.
>
> ii. Calculate or estimate the costs or value of.
>
> iii. Set the value of.

Once you have all the information you need & had a detailed look at your data, it is now time to question the validity of all you have been given. You want to look at those details to be certain they are pertinent or even vital to the situation at hand. You have taken the effort of brainstorming your thoughts, ideas & a list of the facts.

The steps get easier & quicker from here, because we are basically going to look over the data we have, the potential ideas we have discovered & the confirm the decisions we may have made, just not made & stamped; FINAL!

Look over your data once again & apply it to your decisions.

Whether this information & decisions are relative to the scenario you find yourself in is vital at this stage. If you can eliminate data as invalid, your dilemma becomes easier to solve. Irrelevant information once eliminated leaves you with only factual data relative to the situation at hand.

I think of an expression here...

Once you eliminate the impossible, whatever remains, no matter how improbable, must be the truth. ~ Sir Arthur Conan Doyle

Armed with this data, you are now ready to take it another step further. You can begin to calculate the risks or costs associated with any Actions or decisions to be made.

You want to be certain just what it is you are faced with, exactly what the information is telling you. You want to be sure you do not overlook anything. Moving forward will be difficult if you are uncertain about the information you have compiled or what that information is telling you.

Determine just what it is that you have…

What does the information tell you? Get it all down on paper, sticky notes, a spreadsheet, a mind-map or some other source that helps you look at this data rationally. Looking at your information objectively gives you a snapshot of your situation. You may be better prepared for the next step.

The reason you Assess your situation is to know what position you are in before you make any moves. The more detailed the information you have, the easier it becomes to make decisions. We have a clearer picture; it is time to decide.

Chapter 18

Step 8: Adjudicate -

     i. Make a formal judgement or decision about a problem or disputed matter.

    ii. Pronounce or declare (judicially)

Looking to move forward?

Do so with the confidence that you are taking the right steps. With the work you have done, you can be confident that you are making the right decisions.

You have Assessed your situation, calculated all the data, now is the time to make that decision.

You know what to do, that is what the previous steps were for…a build up to that moment when you could know with some degree of certainty, that you could step forth knowing that you might not lose it all on this one…lol. Just kidding, but you can now move forth confidently.

You are armed with facts & information that will help you take the right Action.

Ultimately decide on a course of Action. NOW IS THE TIME! You may not be certain, no one ever is. You may still be wary, there is nothing wrong with that, but you have done your due diligence. If you hesitate too long, the opportunity may pass.

These 10 Constructive Steps may take you further than you imagined possible. You have Analyzed your current or immediate circumstances & your immediate future, but you will need to perform these steps again if you hope to have successful Outcomes, not just one moment. That should be your focus for now…learning to control this 10 Step process on the Outcomes you want to Achieve

Your future is never certain, even with these steps you have taken. But having done these steps, you have the potential to Achieve any Outcomes you Desire.

Now that you have made that decision, make it a firm commitment & resolve in taking your next step. This is the time for you. You have reached that stage for the ultimate culmination of these steps. If these steps were an Actual stairwell you would be at the top.

Move forward with confidence & certainty that you are on solid ground. You are prepared for what may come next.

Decide quickly! Move with certainty! A solid commitment is required & easily made knowing that you are very likely to succeed.

Chapter 19

Step 9: Action -

a. Noun - Action

    i.   The fact or process of doing something, typically to <u>Achieve</u> an aim.

    ii.   The way in which something such as a chemical has an effect or influence.

    iii.   Armed conflict

    iv.   a military engagement

    v.   The events represented in a story or play

    vi.   excited or notable Activity

b.

    i.   a thing done; an Act

    ii.   a legal process

    iii.   a gesture or movement

c.

    i.   A manner or style or doing something, typically the way in which a mechanism works, or a person moves.

    ii.   the mechanism that makes a machine or instrument work.

You see I documented all the definitions here. I have done so to demonstrate that each of these definitions refers to something happening. Something must be done. An Action is movement in any direction. The work you have done ensures that any Actions you take will result in a Positive Outcomes.

Act with certainty. Nothing happens without Action. Nothing will ever be accomplished if you do nothing. Action is the key ingredient to ALL accomplishment. If you have any Desire for success, money or happiness, the way to get it is to do something! Do what it takes to Achieve your Dreams.

If you do nothing, you will Achieve nothing.

"Intention is the starting point of every Dream." ~ Deepak Chopra

Now you know your intentions.

Take that Action! NOW! Take these steps as they are laid out. Once again, you may not need to use all of them. Certainly not every time but in the beginning you should, to gain the skills of using this tool. Being armed with a tool like this one can only enhance the potential for a successful Outcomes.

Take heed of the words within the pages of this book, carry them with you & take heart, knowing that you can Achieve the Outcomes you Desire. I do have a 10 Pg. Report for shorter version with just the 10 Steps…Not so much crap about me. Building a LIFE, you LOVE to LIVE does not come without effort but using tools that will help you such as these 10 steps plus the bonus tools, the SWOT analysis, if done alone, will bring you tremendous value. (psst, you can't do it alone, without previous steps of collecting data)

Best of intentions can only lead to the best of Outcomes with the implementation of many of the steps you find here. I truly hope that I have demonstrated the value of these steps. Practice makes permanent, so believe in yourself & the Desires you possess.

If you want it & if you work at it, you will have it. If you use the steps provided here. Your LIFE & the Outcomes you Desire will be pleasant & Positive.

If you want it…If work for it, you will Build a LIFE you LOVE to LIVE!

Chapter 20

Step 10: Ask -

        i.   say something in order to obtain an answer or some information.

        ii.   request (someone) to do or give something.

Here is another bonus step that I discovered after I had "completed" the book. It was given to me by two of the biggest names in personal development; Mark Victor Hansen & Jack Canfield of *Chicken Soup for the Soul.*

It was when the 8 Steps became 10. I truly believe that we would have entirely different Outcomes without these final 2 steps. I wanted to show you how the 8 Steps became 10, after adding Attitude & Ask after the book was written. After I thought they were complete. They did not become steps, nor could they be considered a program until these 2 extra steps were added.

You will see why they describe this as Aladdin's Lamp. This technique will allow you to move further than you would have thought possible. It allows for not only you to Act, but for others to Act on your behalf.

This gives you exponential growth toward your goals or Outcomes. It gives you leverage that would have been previously unattainable, regardless of all the work you have done to reach this point. Oh, you might Achieve your Outcomes, but you would do it alone.

"If you want to go fast, go alone. If you want to go far, go together." ~ African Proverb.

Aladdin's Genie from the lamp asks him one question. "What do you want?"

Upon making a wish, or asking for what he wants, the genie then replies, "Your wish is my command."

While asking offers no certainty that you will get what you want or even receive a Positive response, it does offer the leverage of others that would not be available if you chose not to ask & you most surely would go alone.

It means you would go faster, but have you ever heard the term, "Going nowhere, fast."

Without the aid of others whom you are free to ask what you want from them. If you choose to ask, they can now provide, if it is also in-line with their purpose.

That is one of the keys to making this work. Unlike the genie, the people you ask are not under any rules or orders that they must obey your wishes. They have free-will & can make any choice that suits their need.

Therefore, you should seek out those that are working toward similar goals or Outcomes. That way you are building upon what you want, by getting them along on your journey, because they are more likely to get what they want. Sell them on your purpose or vision & the value it could hold for them.

If you want to get what you want. After all, you have done so much work toward that result, that it would be a shame not to ask others who would be interested in providing you with greater leverage because it is to their advantage to do so.

Just like Action, if you do not ask, nothing happens. You get no results. If you want help, & most of us do, then you have to ask for it. No one is going to realize that you need help. Even if they were aware you need something, they still would not know the specific type of help you need.

Only by putting it out there, letting the Universe know what you want & then maybe more specifically the people who you would seek aid from, will you have any hope of receiving the support you need.

Ask & ye shall receive! You may have heard this statement before. Take it to heart. If you want to receive anything, then ask for what you want. Ask those who would be able to get what you want. Ask those you want assistance from. Ask for specific help or just basic assistance from those who are able to bring you closer to your Dreams.

I already mentioned that you absolutely cannot accomplish anything substantial by yourself. Ask those who might be able to help you, especially if you believe there is a chance that they might be willing to offer their help.

Chapter 21

Build a LIFE you LOVE to LIVE!

You have now taken many steps necessary to achieving the LIFE of your Dreams. You are now prepared to move forward with the confidence that you can Build a LIFE you LOVE to LIVE.

Your Positive **Attitude** suggests that you will have the confidence to grow strong in achieving the LIFE you Desire.

You have become **aware** of who you are, what you want & you now know how to get it. Especially since you have **accepted** that you are 100% responsible for the Outcomes in your LIFE.

Now you may feel at ease with **acquiescing** to the stress & frustration that you have **Ascertained** all the pertinent or irrelevant information that arms you with facts that will help you grow strong.

That is why you have gone so far as to seek out all the facts you could obtain & **Assess** that information for usefulness & viability to deliver options that you must now **Analyze** for strong options that will let you **Adjudicate** quickly & with certainty that you will get what you want.

Now that you have done all this work, you are armed & ready to strike with confidence knowing that you have the intelligence to take certain **Action**. Don't hesitate to **ask** for support, guidance or leverage from those that will take you beyond your current understanding progress you toward the Outcomes you Desire. Here I offer you one final bonus 'A'. I discovered it as I was writing this book. This one has been documented throughout the book. It has been written down in these pages so often that it should be implanted in your mind, so deeply in fact that it has now entered your subconscious.

Remember I told you that All-important word so vital it appears at the beginning & the end of our process, that first step we started with...ATTITUDE. It comes as a general reminder that a Positive Attitude is so important to our success that we will not Achieve the same results without it.

"Your mental Attitude attracts to you everything that makes you what you are." ~ Napoleon Hill

Without a Positive Attitude you are likely to make negative decisions or Actions. With the entire point of growing & becoming better, you are trying to change things from a negative to a Positive. Your Attitude is the starting point of everything you are trying to Achieve. You want your LIFE to become better. You are trying to Achieve a Positive Outcomes.

If you picked up this book. If you have read it to the end, then you are working to improve your LIFE. Your Attitude is the key ingredient to your Outcomes. Those Outcomes can be Positive or negative depending on the input you offer.

If you had a Positive Attitude from the start, then you had that advantage before you started. If you just jumped to the end of this book & only read this last section, then I have done justice in writing all these words in the book just by reiterating the value of adjusting your Attitude from the start. It also bears repeating over & again that I could not overstate the importance of a Positive Attitude.

A Positive Attitude whenever you can maintain it, can be a game-changer. Every moment of your LIFE could be happy, joyful & satisfactory with a Positive Attitude. If you do not possess that Attitude at this stage, go back & start with that. Work on your Attitude, then begin this work again. I promise that you will Achieve satisfactory Outcomes for most instances you encounter.

Here again are those 10 Steps to Achieve any Outcomes you Desire.

Now that you have taken some study of the steps, they will help guide you to a more certain path with Outcomes you Desire. You will be able to Achieve your Dreams with the tools provided within this book in addition to the 10 Steps we have offered you.

Congratulations!

Keep these steps handy, put them in a notebook, on a small card, the back of a business card, on an app in your phone, so that you can refer to them as often as you might need the 10 Steps to Achieve any Outcomes you Desire!

10 Steps to Achieve any Outcome you Desire

- o **Attitude**
- o **Awareness**
- o **Acceptance**
- o **Acquiesce**
- o **Ascertain**
- o **Assess**
- o **Analyze**
- o **Adjudicate**
- o **Action**
- o **Ask**

Armed with these 10 A's to Achievement you now have control over the power that will allow you to Build a LIFE you LOVE to LIVE!

Thank you for taking the time to learn these 10 Steps. They have been carefully thought out. These steps as they have been created to help you Build a LIFE you LOVE to LIVE are part of a larger program taught by the Author.

RJ Horner; Facilitator, LIVE & LOVE LIFE

For more information about the program, please visit our website: www.live-love-life.ca/10-steps

Email: rjhorner@live-lovve-life.ca

For more information

10 Steps Resources

<u>(Insert Links)</u>

10 Steps FREE Report:

10 Steps Cheat Sheet:

10 Steps Program Upgrades

- o Zoom Weekly
- o 1-on-1 Coaching
- o FULL PACKAGE; Special Price

LIVE & LOVE LIFE Resources:

FB Group:
https://www.facebook.com/groups/454234745401853

FB Page:
https://www.facebook.com/live.love.life.2020

Podcast: https://www.livelovelife.buzzsprout.com/

Website: https://www.live-love-life.ca

Made in the USA
Las Vegas, NV
06 March 2025

19172997R00066